Land of Liberty

Nebraska

W0006637

by Sandra J. Christian,
M.Ed.

Consultant:
Karen Stanley
President
Nebraska State Council
for Social Studies

Capstone
press
Mankato, Minnesota

Capstone Press
151 Good Counsel Drive • P.O. Box 669 • Mankato, Minnesota 56002
http://www.capstone-press.com

Library of Congress Cataloging-in-Publication Data
Christian, Sandra J.
    Nebraska / by Sandra J. Christian.
    p. cm.—(Land of liberty)
    Includes bibliographical references (p. 61) and index.
    ISBN 0-7368-2185-6 (hardcover)
    1. Nebraska—Juvenile literature. [1. Nebraska.] I. Title. II. Series.
F666.3.C48 2004
978.2—dc21   2002156122

Summary: An introduction to the geography, history, government, politics,
    economy, resources, people, and culture of Nebraska, including maps, charts,
    and a recipe.

Editorial Credits
Megan Schoeneberger, editor; Jennifer Schonborn, series designer; Linda Clavel,
book designer; Enoch Peterson, illustrator; Alta Schaffer, photo researcher; Eric
Kudalis, product planning editor

Photo Credits
Cover images: Chimney Rock National Historic Site, UNICORN Stock
Photos/Frank Helberg; soybeans in rows, Visuals Unlimited/Inga Spence

AP/Wide World Photos/Nick Ut, 38; Capstone Press/Gary Sundermeyer, 54; Cheryl
R. Richter, 42–43, 50; Corbis/Bettmann, 29, 34; courtesy of Kenneth Dewey, 15;
Digital Vision, 57; Getty Images/Hulton Archive, 24; Houserstock/Dave G. Houser,
10; John Elk III, 14, 32–33, 40, 46, 63; National Archives Great Lakes Region
(Chicago), 30; NEBRASKAland Magazine/Nebraska Game and Parks Commission
photo, 4; North Wind Picture Archives, 27; One Mile Up Inc., 55 (both); Oregon
Trail Museum Association, 22–23, 58; PhotoDisc Inc., 1; State Historical Society of
North Dakota/photo ID #A5128, 20; Stock Montage Inc., 28; Stock Montage
Inc./The Newberry Library, 18; Timepix/Ted Kirk, 52–53; Tom Till, 8, 13; U.S.
Postal Service, 59; Visuals Unlimited/Daniel D. Lamoreux, 44; Visuals Unlimited/F.
H. Kolwicz, 56; Visuals Unlimited/William J. Weber, 16–17

Artistic Effects
Corbis, Digital Vision, PhotoDisc Inc.

1 2 3 4 5 6 08 07 06 05 04 03

Table of Contents

At Ashfall Fossil Beds State Historical Park, archaeologists show visitors the partially uncovered bones of ancient animals.

Chapter 1

About Nebraska

Millions of years ago, rhinos, camels, and three-toed horses lived in present-day Nebraska. Every day, they crossed the grasslands to a watering hole. There, the animals drank fresh water.

At the same time, nearly 1,000 miles (1,600 kilometers) away in what is now Idaho, a large volcano erupted. Winds blew ash from the volcano across the land to Nebraska. Ash swirled like snowflakes in the air around the watering hole. Huge drifts of ash buried turtles and birds alive.

Herds of horses, camels, and rhinos came to the pond to drink. Ash coated the animals' throats when they breathed. They choked on the thick, dusty air. One by one, they died.

More ash blew around the watering hole and buried it for millions of years. In 1971, a scientist found a white bone sticking up from the ground. He dug deeper and found the rest of the skeleton of a young rhino. Since then, scientists have found many animal skeletons buried in the ash.

Today, visitors can come to the site of the old watering hole near O'Neill in northeastern Nebraska. The park was named Ashfall Fossil Beds State Historical Park. At the park, visitors can see the bones of a three-toed horse, a female rhino with an unborn calf, and many other interesting animals.

The Cornhusker State

Today, farms and cities have replaced most of Nebraska's grasslands. Farmland covers most of the state. Corn, the largest crop, has earned the state its nickname, the Cornhusker State. Removing the outer covering of an ear of corn is called husking. More than 1.5 million people call the Cornhusker State home.

Nebraska's Cities

Nebraska is one of the upper plains states. South Dakota lies to the north. The Missouri River flows for 450 miles (724 kilometers) along Nebraska's border, separating it from Iowa and Missouri to the east. Kansas and Colorado lie to the south. Wyoming is located to the west.

Wind and rain have carved away rocks in Toadstool Geologic Park in northern Nebraska. Early explorers saw the rocky land in this area and called it "the Great American Desert."

Chapter 2

Land, Climate, and Wildlife

Early American explorers thought Nebraska was a desert. In 1806, explorer Zebulon Pike visited the area. He saw bare, dry land. He compared it to African deserts. In 1820, Stephen H. Long called the area "the Great American Desert."

Nebraska is not really a desert at all. It has rich soil for farming. Wetlands, lakes, and rivers help crops and other plants grow well in many parts of the state.

The Great Plains

The Great Plains area covers most of Nebraska. It has three parts. In northern Nebraska is the Sand Hills region.

The High Plains and the Loess Plains make up the rest of the Great Plains in Nebraska.

In northern Nebraska, the Sand Hills covers nearly 20,000 square miles (51,800 square kilometers). The Sand Hills is the largest area of sand dunes in North America.

Grasses grow in the Sand Hills. The grasses keep the sand from blowing away. Water from wetlands, lakes, and streams keeps the grasses from drying out. Farmers let cattle graze on the grasses of this area.

The High Plains area is west and north of the Sand Hills. Water and wind have worn away much of the High Plains.

Grasses grow in the Sand Hills in northern Nebraska. Water from nearby lakes keeps the soil moist.

Nebraska's Land Features

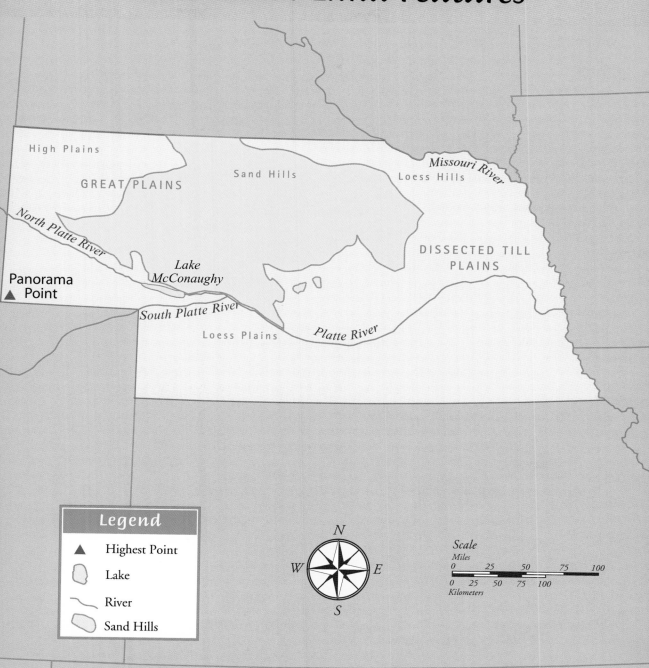

High Plains

GREAT PLAINS

Sand Hills

Loess Hills

Missouri River

North Platte River

Lake McConaughy

DISSECTED TILL PLAINS

Panorama Point

South Platte River

Loess Plains

Platte River

Legend

▲ Highest Point

⬡ Lake

〜 River

⬭ Sand Hills

N
W E
S

Scale
Miles
0   25   50   75   100
0   25   50   75   100
Kilometers

The land is bare except for steep hills and unusual rock formations. Toadstool Geologic Park in northwestern Nebraska has many narrow pillars of rock. Some of these pillars have caps on top, making them look like toadstool mushrooms. The High Plains also shares part of the Badlands with South Dakota.

A small area of the Great Plains is covered by windblown dust called loess. Rainwater collects in the low-lying Loess Plains. Another name for the Loess Plains is the Rainwater Basin. The wetlands in this area attract many birds.

The Dissected Till Plains

The Dissected Till Plains takes up only one-fifth of Nebraska. During the Ice Age, glaciers covered this area. The glaciers trapped soil. When they melted, the glaciers left behind rich soil called till. Over time, streams cut through the land. Ridges and hills break up, or dissect, the till.

Chimney Rock

As early pioneers traveled west, they noted a strange rock formation. The rock jutting about 300 feet (90 meters) into the sky reminded them of a chimney. They called it Chimney Rock. It became a landmark along the Oregon Trail. Many pioneers mentioned this memorable rock in their journals.

The northern part of the Dissected Till Plains is called the Loess Hills. In this area, wind scattered loess across rolling hills.

Plants grow well in the Dissected Till Plains. Farmers grow corn to feed their cattle. Beef cattle also graze on grass that grows in the rich soil.

Rivers and Lakes

Nebraska has more miles or kilometers of rivers than any other state. The main river in Nebraska is the Platte River. It begins in the city of North Platte, where the North Platte and South Platte Rivers come together. It crosses Nebraska from west to east, emptying into the Missouri River.

Nebraska has about 2,500 small lakes. The Sand Hills area has hundreds of shallow natural lakes. When Nebraskans built the Kingsley Dam on the North Platte River, water pooled up behind the dam and formed Lake McConaughy. At about 55 square miles (142 square kilometers), it is the largest lake in Nebraska.

Climate

Nebraska's weather changes often. Rainfall amounts change, bringing flooding one year and drought the next. Hailstorms, thunderstorms, and tornadoes happen quickly when hot air

Huge, dark clouds and thunderstorms often build up over Nebraska's flat land.

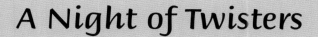

A Night of Twisters

On June 3, 1980, seven huge tornadoes hit Grand Island, Nebraska. On radar, this storm looked like a hurricane. The storm traveled only 5 miles (8 kilometers) per hour. For three hours, the storm stayed over Grand Island.

The storm was strong. It struck with winds of more than 200 miles (322 kilometers) per hour. The entire storm was more than 10 miles (16 kilometers) wide. Five people died, and about 200 people were hurt. The cost of the storm's damage was nearly $300 million.

and cold air meet on the Great Plains. These storms can sometimes break windows, take off roofs, and rip trees from the ground.

Nebraska's winters are mostly snowy. Blizzards with high winds whip snow across the flat land. Western Nebraska receives more snow than the rest of the state. The area gets about 30 inches (76 centimeters) of snow each year.

In southeastern Nebraska, as little as 9 inches (23 centimeters) of snow has fallen in one winter.

Nebraska's Wildlife

Pheasants, prairie chickens, wild turkeys, and other birds thrive on the plains. Many waterfowl and shorebirds use Nebraska waters during fall and spring migrations.

Many other animals make their homes in Nebraska. White-tailed deer, mule deer, elk, and other animals live

in Nebraska. Bighorn sheep live in the High Plains. Bobcats, foxes, and other small animals are also common. Beavers build homes along rivers and lakes. Bass, carp, and trout swim in Nebraska's lakes.

Nebraska's wildlife has changed over time. Before settlers came to the area, huge herds of American bison grazed the plains. Some herds contained more than 10 million bison. Hunters killed large numbers of bison. Today, only a few bison remain.

Thousands of sandhill cranes stop along the Platte River every year as they migrate. Bird lovers gather near the city of Kearney to watch the cranes.

American Indians began using Spanish horses to hunt bison in the 1500s.

Chapter 3

History of Nebraska

American Indians have lived in the Nebraska area for many years. The Pawnee lived in the central part of the state. They built large villages along rivers and hunted bison on the Great Plains. The Omaha, Ponca, and Oto tribes came to eastern Nebraska from the south and east. They lived along the Missouri River. The Lakota, Arapaho, Cheyenne, and other tribes crossed the Missouri River into the area.

The Arrival of Explorers

The lives of the American Indians changed when Spanish explorers came to the area. In 1541, Francisco Vásquez de Coronado claimed southwestern North America for Spain.

Spanish explorers rode through the area on horseback. The American Indians in the area learned about horses from the Spaniards. They began using Spanish horses to hunt bison. With horses, it was easier to haul bison back to their villages.

The French were the next people to explore the area. René-Robert Cavelier, known as Sieur de La Salle, traveled from the north down the Mississippi River in 1682. He claimed the land west of the river and called it the Louisiana Territory after King Louis XIV of France.

Manuel Lisa was a fur trader who built a fort near the Missouri River in the 1800s.

Fur traders followed explorers into Nebraska. French traders came to the Platte River area in the early 1700s. In 1739, traders Pierre and Paul Mallet became the first white settlers to cross Nebraska.

Control of Nebraska

Both Spain and France claimed the Nebraska area. In 1720, Spain sent a group of soldiers led by Pedro de Villasur to reclaim the land. But the Pawnee Indians, France's allies, attacked and killed most of the Spanish soldiers.

Control of the Nebraska area changed often over the next 80 years. In 1763, as part of an agreement to end war in Europe, France gave the land west of the Mississippi River to Spain. In 1800, France forced Spain to return the Louisiana Territory. In 1803, the United States bought the land from France for about $15 million. This sale was called the Louisiana Purchase. The Nebraska area became part of the United States.

In the early 1800s, Manuel Lisa built a fort by the Missouri River. Fur traders from across Nebraska brought beaver skins to trade at Fort Lisa.

The Oregon Trail and the Great Migration

By the early 1840s, the United States' borders stretched to the Pacific Ocean. The government opened the California and Oregon Territories. It offered land to those willing to build farms and homes on the land.

Traveling on foot, on horseback, or in wagons was the main way for settlers to reach these new western territories. Pioneers followed fur traders' trails across Nebraska. All trails followed the Platte River at some point. Pioneers called the

river the Great Platte River Road. The Oregon Trail and the Bozeman Trail were the two most-used trails.

Explorer John Frémont and his wife, Jessie Benton Frémont, became well known for their journeys along the Oregon Trail in 1842 and 1843. Jessie wrote stories that made trips to the West seem like adventures. Readers in the East thought it would be fun to travel west. Thousands of pioneers headed west. This westward movement across Nebraska became known as the Great Migration.

Most settlers used covered wagons to travel west to the California and Oregon Territories.

Becoming a Territory

In the 1840s, most pioneers did not stop in the Nebraska area. Nebraska was Indian Territory. The U.S. Congress signed treaties and passed laws so people could not claim land in Indian Territory. Fort Kearny and the town of Bellevue were the only exceptions. Fort Kearny was built to protect settlers as they traveled across Nebraska. The government also used the fort to make sure settlers did not build homes in Indian Territory. The fort was near the present-day city of Kearney.

At Fort Kearny, soldiers made sure settlers did not stay in Indian Territory.

24

Lawmakers soon changed their minds. They thought the Great Platte River Road would be a good route for a railroad across the continent. Others wanted the Nebraska area to become a territory so that white settlers could claim land west of the Missouri River.

The U.S. Congress argued about whether the new territory would allow slavery. At the time, most southern states wanted the right to own slaves. Most northern states wanted to end slavery.

After 10 years, lawmakers passed the Kansas-Nebraska Act. This law stated that the people of Kansas and the people of Nebraska would decide if their own territory would allow slavery. In 1854, the Kansas-Nebraska Act officially created the Kansas and Nebraska territories.

Civil War

Even after Nebraska became a territory, political troubles continued. Congress was afraid votes in each territory would change the balance of slave states and free states. If Nebraska, Kansas, and other territories chose to be free states, southern states might be outvoted. People in southern states feared they would lose the right to keep slaves.

The U.S. government was unable to solve the issue of slavery peacefully. The mixed feelings about slavery began to move the country closer to war. The Civil War (1861–1865) began when southern states left the Union and formed the Confederate States of America. Northern states fought the Confederacy to try to regain control of the government.

Statehood

The Civil War delayed Nebraska's statehood. When the North won the war in 1865, lawmakers had to change parts of the state's constitution. The constitution could no longer say that only "free, white males" could vote. After allowing freed male slaves the right to vote, Nebraska became the 37th state on March 1, 1867. That same year, the village of Lancaster became the capital. Nebraskans renamed the city Lincoln after President Abraham Lincoln.

The new state faced conflicts with American Indians. In 1869, the Ogalala Sioux signed a treaty with the United States. The United States agreed to stop using the Bozeman Trail. The Ogalala and Lakota Sioux agreed to leave Nebraska and move to what is now South Dakota. Many Sioux refused to leave the land of their ancestors. They continued fighting until Lakota

Sioux Chief Crazy Horse surrendered in northwestern Nebraska on May 6, 1877. Nearly all American Indians were then forced to move to present-day Oklahoma.

Grasshoppers and Drought

At first, Nebraska's settlers struggled. From 1874 to 1877, swarms of grasshoppers came to Nebraska's farmlands. These gnawing insects ate oat, barley, corn, and wheat crops. Many settlers gave up and left.

By the 1880s, railroad companies built lines that crossed Nebraska. The companies paid for advertisements in the East

SALT CREEK, AT ASHLAND, NEB.—LOOKING TOWARD THE PLATTE HILLS, FROM THE MILL HILL.
BURLINGTON AND MISSOURI RIVER RAILROAD.
Iowa and Nebraska Lands for Sale, on 10 Years Credit,

Railroad companies printed ads to attract settlers to Nebraska.

and even in Europe. The ads described the great farmlands of Nebraska. Many people saw the ads and traveled to the state.

Drought and low prices for farm products caused farmers to lose money. With the Reclamation Act of 1902, the U.S. government built irrigation systems in Nebraska and other western states. Settlers started growing winter wheat, alfalfa, and sugar beets on the dry, grassy land.

In 1904, the U.S. Congress passed the Kinkaid Act. This act made 640-acre (259-hectare) homesteads available to people settling in western Nebraska. The population in western Nebraska grew.

Early Nebraskan families stacked blocks of sod to build homes. They called the houses "soddies."

Father Flanagan

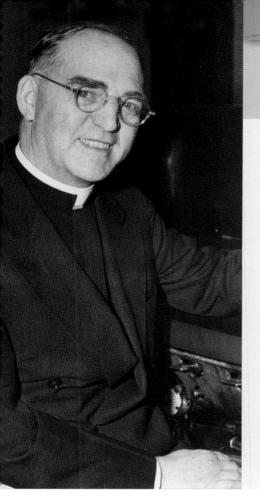

In the early 1900s, Father Edward J. Flanagan of Omaha became worried about the lives of orphaned or neglected young boys. The boys often fought with others and broke laws.

Father Flanagan believed he could help these boys. On December 12, 1917, he opened Boys Town, a home for neglected boys from across the country. Father Flanagan welcomed any boy who needed a loving home.

Since 1979, Boys Town has welcomed girls as well as boys. Today, the Girls and Boys Town organization offers homes for troubled youth.

For a few years, rains were plentiful. Crops were successful. But droughts soon hit, and the land became hard and cracked. Planting was impossible. Many farmers gave up. They sold their homesteads and left western Nebraska.

World War I and the Great Depression

Nebraskans helped their country when the United States joined World War I (1914–1918) in 1917. Nebraska gave about $300 million to help pay war costs. Nebraskans bought more war stamps than any other state. War stamps raised money for the armed forces. Plenty of rain and good growing seasons helped Nebraska grow farm products to help feed the country during the war.

Following World War I, Nebraska's economy suffered. By the time of the Great Depression (1929–1939), farm prices fell. At the same time, another severe drought dried out the Great Plains. Winds blew thick dust storms over the land.

The Hastings Naval Ammunition Depot made 40 percent of the ammunition used in World War II.

Once again, many farmers could not pay their bills and had to give up their land.

Improving Nebraska

In the 1930s, the U.S. government helped Nebraska improve the state's economy. The U.S. government began a program called the New Deal. Nebraska farmers could borrow money from the government. Borrowing this money helped them keep their farms.

World War II

During World War II (1939–1945), factories in Nebraska made war equipment. Nebraskans built three weapons plants. Factories in Nebraska made more than $1.2 billion worth of bombs, bullets, airplanes, and other war equipment.

Nebraska also supplied farm products to the country during World War II. Ranchers raised cattle. Farmers grew large amounts of corn, potatoes, oats, and wheat. Farm products eased war-related food shortages.

Did you know...?
During World War II, Fort Robinson in Nebraska trained dogs as part of the "K-9 Corps." The dogs saved soldiers' lives by warning them of hidden enemies and delivering messages between troops.

After World War II

In the years after World War II, farming in Nebraska changed. Nebraskan farmers began using modern machinery and farming methods. Fewer farm workers were needed to run a farm.

In the early 1980s, the economy across the country worsened. Land values in Nebraska dropped, and many farmers took out large loans. Farmers who could not pay back their

loans lost their land. To help the economy, the Nebraska legislature passed tax breaks for farms and businesses in 1987. These businesses created new jobs in Nebraska.

Today, many people have moved from farms to cities. Lincoln, Omaha, and other large Nebraska cities have many businesses. Rural communities have drawn new industries to their towns.

Omaha, Nebraska, is home to many insurance and financial companies, including Mutual of Omaha. This company has more than 6,000 workers.

Senator George W. Norris represented Nebraska at the U.S. Capitol in Washington, D.C. He also persuaded Nebraskans to use a unicameral state legislature.

Chapter 4

Government and Politics

Until the 1930s, Nebraska's lawmakers met in two groups. New laws needed to be passed by both the senate and the house of representatives.

U.S. Senator George W. Norris from Nebraska believed the state government did not need two groups. He told Nebraskans that having just one group would make government easier to understand. He also told them that having two groups of lawmakers cost a great deal of money. Nebraska could save money by having only one group.

Many Nebraskans were ready for a change. In 1934, they voted to change their government to a one-house system.

" . . . there is no sense or reason in having the same thing done twice, especially if it is to be done by two bodies of men elected in the same way and having the same jurisdiction."

—George W. Norris, former U.S. Senator from Nebraska

This system is called a unicameral legislature. Nebraska's first one-house legislature met on January 5, 1937.

Running only one legislative house saved time and money. The last two-house session began in 1935 and lasted 110 days. The session cost taxpayers $202,593. The first unicameral session two years later lasted 98 days. It cost only $103,445, even though lawmakers passed 22 more bills. Today, Nebraska is the only state that uses the one-house system.

Political Parties

Nebraska's state legislature is different in another way. In all other states, the ballot lists the candidates' political parties. Voters often choose candidates in a certain party. Since 1937, the Nebraska ballot has not shown if candidates are Democrats, Republicans, Independents, or members of any other political party. Nebraskans vote based on the candidates' views on education, taxes, or other issues, not their political parties.

Nebraska's State Government

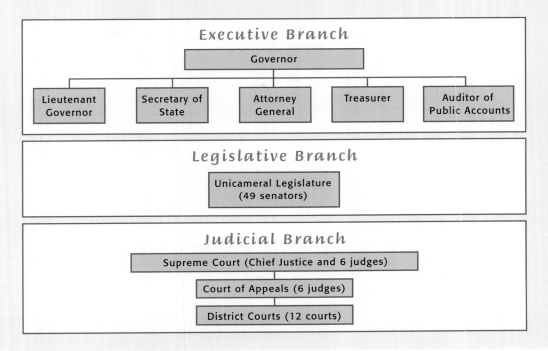

Executive Branch

Governor

- Lieutenant Governor
- Secretary of State
- Attorney General
- Treasurer
- Auditor of Public Accounts

Legislative Branch

Unicameral Legislature (49 senators)

Judicial Branch

Supreme Court (Chief Justice and 6 judges)

Court of Appeals (6 judges)

District Courts (12 courts)

During history, Nebraskans have voted for people who stand for their views, no matter what their political party may be. In the 1890s, many Nebraska farmers switched from the Republican Party to the Populist Party after land prices fell. Populists wanted to change farming laws. From 1895 to 1901, Nebraskans chose Populist governors.

The Executive Branch

The governor leads the executive branch of Nebraska. Voters elect the governor and the lieutenant governor together for four-year terms. Other elected members of the executive branch are the secretary of state, attorney general, treasurer, and auditor.

In 1986, Nebraska's race for governor made national history. Republican Kay Orr and Democrat Helen Boosalis ran for governor. This race was the first time two women had ever

Kay Orr was the first female Republican governor of any state.

"Destiny . . . is not a thing to be waited for. It is a thing to be achieved."
—William Jennings Bryan, three-time Democratic nominee
for U.S. president, who lived in Lincoln

competed for governor of any state. Orr won the election. She became the first female Republican governor in U.S. history.

The Judicial Branch

A supreme court, court of appeals, and 12 district courts make up the judicial branch of Nebraska's government. The supreme court has seven justices who serve six-year terms. Court of appeals judges and district court judges also serve six-year terms.

Choosing a new judge involves Nebraska's governor and Nebraska's voters. First, a committee makes a list of people who would make good judges. They give the names to the governor. The governor makes a choice from the list. After the new judge has worked for three years, his or her name is put on a ballot. Voters decide if they think the judge has done a good job. If voters do not think the judge has done well, the governor chooses a new judge from the list.

Some factories in Nebraska turn locally grown corn into a fuel called ethanol.

Chapter 5

Economy and Resources

When many people think of Nebraska, they think of cornfields and farms. People across the world depend on Nebraska farm products.

Agriculture

Agriculture is the biggest business in Nebraska. Corn is Nebraska's leading crop. For 20 years, the state has led the country in the production of popcorn. In 1999, Nebraska was number one in Great Northern bean production. Other crops in Nebraska are soybeans, wheat, hay, and sugar beets.

In Nebraska, livestock is a $5.5 billion industry. Cattle provide the most farm income. Hogs, sheep, and poultry make up the rest. Nebraska ranks first in the country for commercial livestock slaughter.

Manufacturing

Food processing is a big part of Nebraska's economy. Many types of food products in grocery stores come from Nebraska. Many Nebraska companies pack beef, pork, and poultry. Other companies process corn products, canned and frozen

fruits and vegetables, and potato chips. The Kellogg's cereal company makes cereal in Omaha. The first TV dinners were tested in Nebraska. Today, Swanson frozen dinners are made in Nebraska.

Nebraska has a variety of other manufacturing companies. The Iams factory in Aurora makes dog and cat food. Some factories make paint, cleaning supplies, or plastic bags. Other plants make farm machinery, irrigation systems, and electrical equipment. Goodyear factories in Lincoln and Norfolk make hoses for cars.

Weaver's Snacks, a snack food company in Lincoln, uses machinery to make large amounts of potato chips.

Transportation

As Nebraska grows, the state builds highways, airports, and
railroads. In 1972, Nebraska was the first state to complete
its assigned 478-mile (769-kilometer) section of Interstate
Highway 80 across the United States. In 2000, Nebraska
had 92,791 miles (149,329 kilometers) of public roads and
highways. Nebraska has 269 airports, most of which are small
and privately owned. Eppley Airfield near Omaha is Nebraska's
largest airport. In 2001, 3.7 million passengers passed through
this airport. Several major railroads also cross the state.

Nebraskans planted the
trees in the Nebraska
National Forest.

"Arbor Day is not like other holidays. Each of those reposes on the past, while Arbor Day proposes for the future."
—J. Sterling Morton, founder of Arbor Day, from Nebraska City

Natural Resources

Soil and water are Nebraska's greatest natural resources. Nebraskans work hard to conserve them. Winds and rains can strip away soil. Trees planted on the edges of farmlands block the wind to stop erosion.

Most trees growing in Nebraska were not there when European settlers arrived in the 1800s. Early settlers found wide, grassy plains. They began planting forests to block the wind and provide shade from the hot sun. Today, Nebraska National Forest in Halsey is the only national forest that is entirely hand-planted.

Nebraska has the largest underground freshwater supply in the United States. It is called the Ogalala Aquifer. The aquifer is like a huge sponge that holds water in the rocks below the ground. Many Nebraska farmers use this natural resource to bring water to dry soil. Today, farmers use irrigation on 5.7 million acres (2.3 million hectares) of Nebraska's farmland.

At the Lied Jungle in the Henry Doorly Zoo of Omaha, trails bring visitors close to rich plant life and a tall waterfall.

Chapter 6

People and Culture

Visitors to the Henry Doorly Zoo in Omaha can explore the Lied Jungle, the largest indoor rainforest in the world. This exhibit features animals and plants from rainforests in Asia, Africa, and South America. As visitors cross hanging bridges and explore dark caves, birds and butterflies fly freely from tree to tree. Cool mist falls lightly from the treetops. Visitors can even climb to Danger Point, where a waterfall plunges 50 feet (15 meters) to the water below.

In the zoo's Desert Dome, visitors stand beneath a ceiling of 1,760 clear plastic triangles. Sunlight shines through the plastic ceiling, heating the air. Visitors walk through a cactus forest, where prickly cactus plants grow close together.

"We will travel as far as we can, but we cannot in one lifetime see all that we would like to see or learn all that we hunger to know."
                    —Loren Eiseley, poet and philosopher, born in Lincoln

Many museums in Nebraska showcase the state's history. At the University of Nebraska State Museum, visitors can see the world's largest woolly mammoth fossil, which was found in Nebraska. In Lincoln, Nebraskans learn about their state's history at the Museum of Nebraska History. To learn even more, they can visit the Oregon Trail Museum at Scotts Bluff National Monument or the Homestead National Monument in Beatrice. The Willa Cather Pioneer Memorial in Red Cloud is dedicated to Nebraskan author Willa Cather for her prize-winning books and stories. It is the largest historic district dedicated to an author in the United States.

The People of Nebraska

Nebraska is a rural state. Nearly one-half of Nebraskans live in small towns and farming areas. Omaha and Lincoln are the only major cities with more than 50,000 residents.

Most people in Nebraska have European heritage. Their families traveled to the state from Czechoslavakia, Italy,

Nebraska's Ethnic Backgrounds

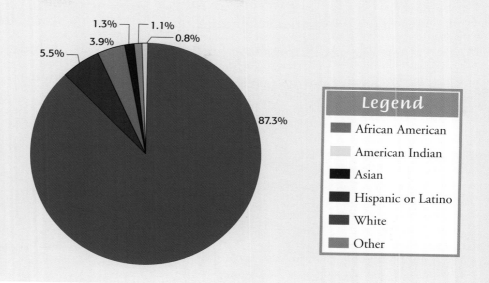

Germany, Sweden, Denmark, Ireland, Spain, and other European countries.

Compared to Europeans, not many African Americans live in Nebraska. After the Civil War, freed slaves came to Nebraska. In 1870, Robert Anderson was the first African American to build a homestead in Box Butte County. By 1900, more than 6,000 African Americans called Nebraska home. Most came to Omaha where jobs were easier to find. Today, most African Americans live in Lincoln or Omaha.

Festivals in towns across Nebraska celebrate the state's heritage. Hispanics celebrate Cinco de Mayo in Scottsbluff. Oakland and Stromsburg hold Swedish festivals in June. Czechs and Slovaks have a festival in Wilber in August.

The Czech and Slovak festival held in Wilber features dancing and people wearing traditional clothing.

The Ponca, Omaha, and Winnebago hold powwows in Nebraska throughout summer. A Danish Christmas in Dannebrog finishes off the year.

Education

Nebraskans take pride in their educational system. In 1963, the state began to broadcast educational TV programming to the entire state. The University of Nebraska has campuses in Lincoln, Omaha, and Kearney. By 2001, Nebraska had 14 public and 24 private colleges and universities.

As more people move from farms to cities, fewer elementary and high school students enroll in rural schools. Schools with fewer students in one town often join together with schools in other towns to make a larger, less expensive school district. A local school might be closed. Students are then bussed to a school in a nearby town.

The Cornhuskers

Nebraska does not have any major league sports teams. Instead, fans cheer for the Cornhuskers from the University of Nebraska.

A memorable Cornhusker football game happened on Thanksgiving Day in 1910. The Cornhuskers played the team from Haskell University in Lawrence, Kansas. The Cornhuskers scored 20 touchdowns, 17 extra points, and one safety. At the time, touchdowns were worth five points. A safety was worth two points. The final score was 119-0.

Cornhusker football games almost always draw huge crowds. Fans dressed in red and white, the team's colors, fill the

76,000 seats in the stadium. Fans have watched the Cornhuskers win many titles and championships.

A Proud State

Once dismissed as the Great American Desert, for nearly 200 years Nebraska has proven it is a state with great worth. From fields of corn to busy cities, the people of Nebraska are proud to live in the Cornhusker State.

Fans fill Memorial Stadium in Lincoln to cheer for the Cornhusker football team.

Recipe: Fruity Cream Pie

The state drink of Nebraska is Kool-Aid. In the early 1900s, Edwin E. Perkins invented a liquid drink mix called Fruit Smack. Perkins found that bottles cost too much to ship, and they often broke. Instead, he found a way to dry out the Fruit Smack and turn it into a powder. In 1927, Kool-Aid was born. The first flavors were strawberry, cherry, lemon-lime, grape, orange, and raspberry. Today, many recipes use powdered drink mix like Kool-Aid. You can use your favorite flavor of powdered drink mix to make this pie.

Ingredients

1 14-ounce (420-gram) can sweetened condensed milk
1 envelope powdered drink mix, any flavor
1 8-ounce (240-gram) carton whipped topping, thawed
1 preformed graham cracker pie crust

Equipment

can opener
medium mixing bowl
rubber spatulas
mixing spoon

What You Do

1. Use a can opener to open the can of sweetened condensed milk.

2. In a medium mixing bowl, combine powdered drink mix and sweetened condensed milk. Use a rubber spatula to get all of the sweetened condensed milk out of the can.

3. Add whipped topping to the drink mix and condensed milk. Mix well with mixing spoon. The mixture will be stiff.

4. Pour mixture into graham cracker crust. Use a rubber spatula to scrape the sides of the bowl and to smooth the top of the pie.

5. Chill the pie in refrigerator for at least 12 hours.

Makes about 8 servings

Nebraska's Flag and Seal

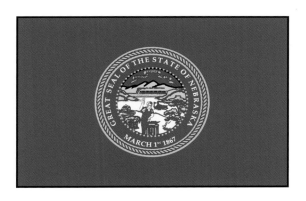

Nebraska's Flag

On Nebraska's flag, the state seal is printed in gold and silver. The background is blue. The state adopted the flag in 1925. Until 1963, the flag was called a banner. In 1963, lawmakers changed the name from banner to flag.

Nebraska's State Seal

When Nebraska became a state, lawmakers created an official state seal. Lawmakers paid $25 to create the seal. The seal shows a farmer with a hammer and anvil. Behind the farmer, a settler's cabin sits near sheaves of wheat and stalks of corn. A steamboat travels on the Missouri River. A train heads toward the Rocky Mountains. The state motto, "Equality before the law," is written on a banner at the top of the seal.

Almanac

General Facts

Nickname: Cornhusker State

Population: 1,711,263 (U.S. Census, 2000)

Population rank: 38th

Capital: Lincoln

Largest cities: Omaha, Lincoln, Bellevue, Grand Island, Kearney

Agriculture

Agricultural products: Beef, hogs, sheep, poultry, corn, soybeans, Great Northern beans, wheat, popcorn

Climate

Average winter temperature: 25 degrees Fahrenheit (minus 4 degrees Celsius)

Average summer temperature: 72 degrees Fahrenheit (22 degrees Celsius)

Average annual precipitation: 23 inches (58 centimeters)

Geography

Area: 77,358 square miles (200,357 square kilometers)

Size rank: 16th

Highest point: Panorama Point, 5,426 feet (1,654 meters)

Lowest point: Missouri River, 480 feet (146 meters)

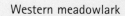

Western meadowlark

Honeybees

Timeline

State History

1541
Francisco Vásquez de Coronado claims southwestern North America for Spain; his group meets the Pawnee, Omaha, Ponca, and other American Indians.

1682
René-Robert Cavelier, known as Sieur de La Salle, claims parts of present-day Nebraska for France.

1720
The Pawnee defeat Pedro de Villasur's Spanish army.

1843
The Great Migration begins.

1854
Congress passes the Kansas-Nebraska Act and creates the Nebraska Territory.

1867
Nebraska becomes the 37th state on March 1.

1917
Father Edward J. Flanagan opens Boys Town.

U.S. History

1620
Pilgrims establish a colony in the New World.

1775–1783
American colonists and the British fight the Revolutionary War.

1803
As part of the Louisiana Purchase, the United States buys the Louisiana Territory, including Nebraska, from France.

1861–1865
The Union and the Confederacy fight the Civil War.

1914–1918
World War I is fought; the United States enters the war in 1917.

58

1934
Nebraska votes to change the state legislature to a one-house system.

1927
Edwin E. Perkins invents Kool-Aid.

1963
Nebraska begins to broadcast educational TV programming to the entire state.

1986
Kay Orr and Helen Boosalis run for governor; this race is the first time two women tried for governor of any state.

1929–1939
The United States experiences the Great Depression.

1964
U.S. Congress passes the Civil Rights Act, which makes discrimination illegal.

2001
On September 11, terrorists attack the World Trade Center and the Pentagon.

1939–1945
World War II is fought; the United States enters the war in 1941.

Words to Know

aquifer (AK-wuh-fuhr)—an underground lake

dissect (di-SEKT)—to cut apart

drought (DROUT)—a long period of time without rainfall

economy (i-KON-uh-mee)—the way state runs its industry, trade, and finance

erosion (e-ROH-zhuhn)—a slow wearing away of soil by water or wind

glacier (GLAY-shur)—a large, slow-moving sheet of ice and snow

homestead (HOME-sted)—in the American West, a piece of land given to a settler by the U.S, government

industry (IN-duh-stree)—a branch of business or trade

irrigation (ihr-uh-GAY-shuhn)—to supply water to crops through ditches, pipes, or streams

loess (LESS)—windblown dust

territory (TAIR-uh-tor-ee)—a large area of land

unicameral (yoo-nuh-KAM-er-uhl)—having a one-house legislature

To Learn More

Bjorklund, Ruth. *Nebraska.* Celebrate the States. New York: Benchmark Books, 2002.

Blashfield, Jean F. *The Oregon Trail.* We the People. Minneapolis: Compass Point Books, 2001.

Flocker, Michael. *Nebraska: the Cornhusker State.* World Almanac Library of the States. Milwaukee: World Almanac Library, 2002.

McNair, Sylvia. *Nebraska.* America the Beautiful. New York: Children's Press, 1999.

Internet Sites

Do you want to find out more about Nebraska?
Let FactHound, our fact-finding hound dog, do the research for you.

Here's how:

1) Visit *http://www.facthound.com*
2) Type in the **Book ID** number:
   0736821856
3) Click on **FETCH IT.**

FactHound will fetch Internet sites picked by our editors just for you!

Places to Write and Visit

Ashfall Fossil Beds State Historical Park
86930 517th Avenue
Royal, NE 68773

Henry Doorly Zoo
3701 South 10th Street
Omaha, NE 68107

Homestead National Monument
8523 W. Highway 4
Beatrice, NE 68310

Office of the Governor
P.O. Box 94848
State Capitol
Lincoln, NE 68509-4848

University of Nebraska State Museum
307 Morrill Hall
University of Nebraska
Lincoln, NE 68588-0338

Willa Cather Pioneer Memorial
413 N. Webster
Red Cloud, NE 68970

The American Institute of Architects declared Nebraska's capitol building to be one of the modern architectural wonders of the world.

Index

T 57142